LEARNING A TRADE, PREPARING FOR A CAREER™

THE VO-TECH
TRACK TO SUCCESS IN
HEALTH CARE

Susan Henneberg

ROSEN
PUBLISHING®

New York

Published in 2015 by The Rosen Publishing Group, Inc.
29 East 21st Street, New York, NY 10010

Library of Congress Cataloging-in-Publication Data

Henneberg, Susan, author.
The vo-tech track to success in health care/Susan Henneberg.—First
edition.
     pages cm.—(Learning a trade, preparing for a career)
Includes bibliographical references and index.
ISBN 978-1-4777-7730-5 (library bound)
1. Medicine—Vocational guidance—Juvenile literature. 2. Allied health
personnel—Vocational guidance—Juvenile literature. I. Title.
R690.H46 2015
610.73'7069—dc23

                                                          2013044062

Manufactured in the United States of America

CONTENTS

INTRODUCTION

Can you imagine yourself saving someone's life? Even more, can you imagine yourself doing this as part of your job? Hundreds of thousands of Americans do every day. These are health care workers. They are doctors, nurses, and emergency medical technicians (EMTs). They are also nursing assistants, X-ray technicians, and home health aides. They work in hospitals, laboratories, and offices. They also work in schools, storefront clinics, and department stores.

From those who attend medical school to those who learn on the job, health care workers at every level help Americans live the best lives possible. They don't do it for the money, though the pay is often good. They don't do it for the job security, though that is good as well. Health care workers feel passionate about what they do. They work long hours under stressful conditions. However, with that work comes the satisfaction of knowing they help people live long, healthy, productive lives. Does being part of the health care world sound like something you want to do?

Many students want to do something with their lives that will make a difference in the lives of others. A health care career can help them achieve that goal. There are many challenges in the health care field. The jobs can be physically and emotionally demanding. Students need to be competent in math and science.

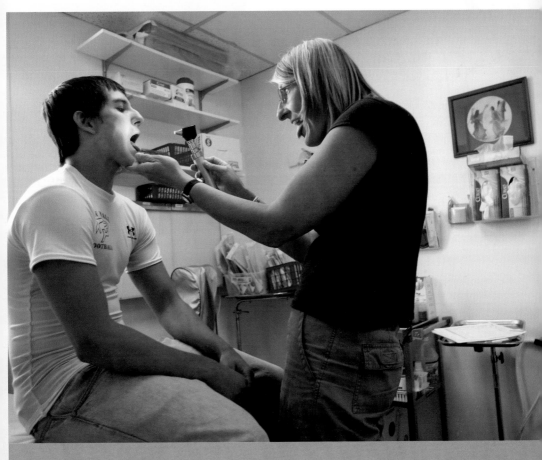

Health care workers provide essential services to their communities, such as conducting physicals, diagnosing diseases, and saving lives.

However, there are many rewards. A wide variety of jobs are available. These jobs are predicted to be plentiful. Health care workers often make higher-than-average wages. They can count on job security. These workers also have the knowledge that they are contributing to the well-being of the population.

Students in most communities around the country can begin preparing for a career in health care while still in high school. States and school districts are seeing an increased demand for career-focused education. They are developing vocational-technical programs and career academies. For many teens, enrolling in a health careers program is a great way to start preparing for the future. Some students don't want or can't afford a four-year college degree. High school students who participate in vocational programs in high school often stay in school longer. They are less likely to need remedial classes in college. They save thousands of dollars of college tuition money by completing college classes while still in high school.

Is a career in health care right for you? Are you ready to start preparing now? Then read on because you, like many teens around the country, can begin your future today.

Chapter One

WHY THE HEALTH CARE FIELD NEEDS YOU

So you are thinking of a career in health care. Maybe you know someone who is a nurse or a dental assistant. Maybe your favorite TV show takes place in a busy hospital. Whatever the inspiration, a career in the health care field is worth considering. Here are some of the most important reasons why.

A Huge Need for Health Care Workers

There is an enormous need for health care workers. A 2012 Georgetown University study forecasts that in the coming years, the health care economy will grow twice as fast as the national economy. Why is the health care business growing? There are many reasons. One is the change in the average age of the population. Americans are getting older. People in the baby boomer age group—those born between 1946 and 1964—are becoming seniors. Many health care

One of the fastest-growing fields in the health care industry is geriatrics. It provides great opportunities for those who enjoy interacting with the senior population.

workers in this age group can no longer keep up with the fast pace of their jobs. In some cases, they are moving into desk jobs. Many are also retiring. This is creating a lot of job openings for younger workers.

This large group of older people will also need more health care. The National Center for Health Statistics (NCHS) reported that almost a third of all doctor visits are from people over age sixty-five. Older people are sicker. They have more chronic conditions. The NCHS reported that 57 percent of women over sixty-five have high blood pressure and 56 percent have arthritis. Sixty-five percent of people in this age group need help completing everyday tasks, such as doing housework and making meals. There will be many jobs for health care workers who enjoy working with older people.

Another rise in health care needs comes from military veterans. Injured soldiers from recent wars have put a strain on Veterans Affairs (VA) services. One Harvard University report predicts that 44 percent of returning soldiers will make a medical claim. Many of these servicemen and servicewomen will need therapy to recover from injuries. Many will need mental health care. Some soldiers are returning from active service with post-traumatic stress disorder (PTSD). In 2013, the Department of Veterans Affairs operated the largest health care system in the United States. Health care workers will find many jobs in one of the 1,700 VA hospitals and counseling centers.

New medical technology has created a need for trained technicians. These medical techs work in diagnostics and treatment. Examples of needed techs

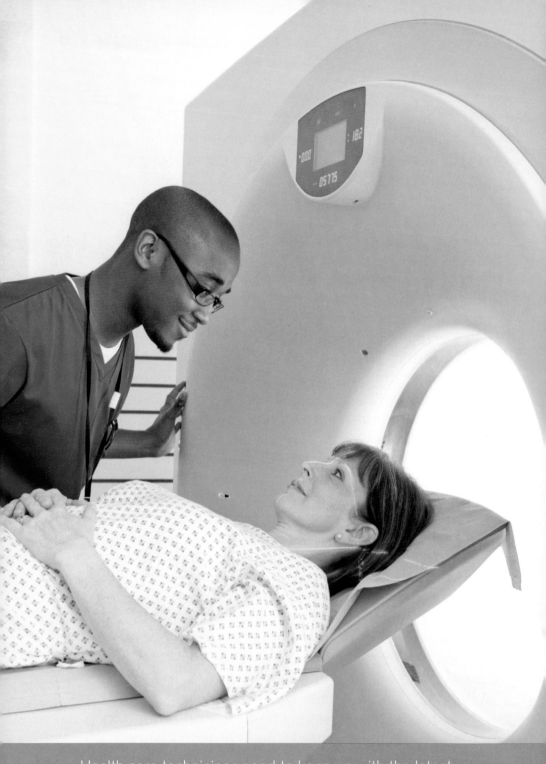

Health care technicians need to keep up with the latest developments in medical technology, such as computed tomography (CT) scans.

are those who work with heart, dialysis, imaging, and ultrasound machines. Some even work with specialized robots. Students who like working with technology can learn how to use this new equipment. Trained information technology (IT) workers will also be needed in the health sector. New health care laws require that patient records be computerized. Health care workers who are adept with technology will find many ways to use their skills.

CERTIFIED NURSING ASSISTANTS

Certified nursing assistants (CNAs) work directly with patients, under the supervision of registered nurses (RNs). They work in many different types of health care sites, including hospitals and long-term care facilities. Some work in patients' homes. They may work day shifts or night shifts.

CNAs take patients' vital signs, including measures of heart rate and blood pressure. They may bathe patients and help with dressing and feeding. They may care for wounds. In many cases, they develop close relationships with their patients. They do important work. This job is considered entry level, and CNAs earn much less than RNs. However, a CNA job can be a first step to a great career.

Advantages of a Health Care Career

Health care workers will find that their skills are in high demand. This has many advantages. Trained and experienced workers will find many job openings. Job shortages typically force employers to offer higher pay. In addition, employers will likely compete for workers by offering better benefits. For example, one hospital might offer more vacation days than another. A company might include a perk such as free parking or paid uniform cleanings. Some employers might even offer sign-on bonuses. This means that they pay a sum of money to a new employee to work for them, rather than for a different organization.

Health care workers will likely find that they have a high level of job security. They will be less likely to be laid off than other workers. Even during the 2007–2009 recession, jobs in health care kept growing.

Health care jobs are among the highest-paying occupations. For example, a nurse with a two-year degree can make as much as a teacher with a four-year degree. Workers who keep up with the latest technology can also make good salaries.

Opportunities in Health Care

One of the biggest advantages of a career in health care is that the field is so broad. There are jobs at every level, from entry-level aides or techs to nurses,

VETERINARY CAREERS

If you love animals, you might want to consider a career as a veterinary assistant, technician, or technologist. They do many tasks for the veterinarian. They weigh animals. They give medications. They clean cages and kennels. They help in surgery. It can be very rewarding to see a pet get well. There is a downside also. Sick animals may bite or scratch. Owners sometimes can't afford to pay for the care their pets need. Sometimes animals need to be put down. It can be hard to see an animal that you have cared for not make it.

A veterinary assistant can learn on the job. A veterinary technician typically earns an associate's degree from a community college. He or she then takes a credentialing exam. A veterinary technologist needs a bachelor's degree. According to the 2013 *Occupational Outlook Handbook*, jobs for veterinary technicians and technologists are expected to increase greatly in the future. You can learn more by volunteering at your local animal shelter. There, you can watch the veterinary technicians and technologists work with the animals.

Veterinary technicians help veterinarians by doing many of the tasks necessary in caring for animals.

doctors, and researchers. One way of categorizing health care positions is by the amount of education needed. Some health care jobs need only a high school diploma. Workers are trained on the job. Higher-level positions may need many years of training beyond college. For example, surgeons must first earn their MD degree. They then study for five or more years to become specialists in surgery.

Another way to categorize health care jobs is by what the workers do. Primary care workers diagnose and treat patients. They are doctors, nurses, and therapists. They are also assistants and aides. Another job category includes specialists in related sciences and technologies. Examples include medical lab technicians, pharmacists, and medical researchers. A third category includes office team members. These workers keep track of records and billing. They keep medical facilities running.

There are a wide variety of places where health care workers work. Hospitals, residential care centers, and outpatient care centers are found in most communities. They offer many jobs for workers at every level. These organizations often work with patients with acute issues. This means that patients need a great deal of care. There are also doctor, dentist, and physical therapy offices. Doctors, nurses, and assistants in these offices all work directly with patients. Health care workers are

Lab technicians, like this dental lab technician, often learn their skills through on-the-job training given by experienced professionals.

also needed in home health care agencies. This is a fast-growing field. Many elder Americans need help with daily life. Finally, medical labs offer many different kinds of health care jobs.

Many jobs for health care workers are located in cities. However, there is also a great need for workers in rural areas. In America's small towns, people sometimes have to travel a long way to get the care they need.

Americans have come to expect the best health care in the world. However, there are challenges in the field as well. First, health care is costly. Wealthy people tend to have the best insurance plans. Poor people are sometimes left with the least access to quality care. Second, health care is centered in cities. Rural areas often lack services beyond basic care. In addition, medical technology changes quickly. Health care workers must often update their skills. Finally, highly educated professionals such as doctors and registered nurses earn high salaries. They are in great demand. But there is a large pay gap between these jobs and paraprofessionals. These are support workers who are trained in offices, hospitals, and community colleges. They work under the direction of professionals and receive a lot less pay.

Despite these issues, a health care career is a great opportunity for the right person. This growing field can offer high wages, job security, and career mobility. Even more important, health care workers feel a lot of satisfaction. They know they are making a difference in the world.

Chapter Two

FINDING THE RIGHT HEALTH CARE CAREER PATH FOR YOU

Some people know from childhood exactly what career they want when they grow up. Others struggle their whole lives to find even a clue. One of the best aspects of the health care field is that a broad variety of skills, talents, and abilities are needed. But how do you know if you have what it takes to be successful in a health care career? You will need to do an honest analysis of yourself. You will need to compare your qualities with those needed in medical jobs. These occupations are rewarding, but they are not for everyone.

What Skills, Characteristics, and Personality Traits Do You Need?

Let's start with some of the character traits that are needed by health care workers at every level. Workers need to be able to control their emotions. Medical careers can be very stressful. People are not at their best when they are sick. They may lash out at those taking care of them. Health care workers need to remain calm and patient under pressure. Are you good at avoiding drama? Do you keep your temper under control when provoked?

Health care workers also need to be detail-oriented. They need to be precise and accurate. Often their tasks have many steps. Think about how you reflect these qualities. Do you complete your schoolwork without a lot of mistakes? Can you go through a long biology lab without errors?

Health care workers need to be organized and methodical. They also need to be good problem solvers. This requires the ability to think both critically and creatively. Health care workers may need to make instant decisions that have serious consequences. They need to do this confidently without getting flustered. How well do you think on your feet? Are you good at making decisions? Or do you prefer to let others decide?

Health care is a team effort. A lot of health care work is fast-paced. It helps if everyone on a team does his or her part. Good

Teamwork skills, such as sharing information and agreeing on solutions, are essential in health care occupations.

team members are dependable. They need to have a strong work ethic. How well do you work in a group? Do you always do your part? Or do you let others pick up the slack?

Amy Harrison hires nursing assistants for a hospital in Iowa. She started as a CNA. She spoke about the traits needed to be successful in an interview on myFootpath.com, a career Web site. "If you don't think highly of yourself, you're probably not going to feel like taking care of anyone else," Harrison said. "You need to be dependable, a team player, and take pride in your career."

People are born with certain personality traits. However, skills can be developed over time. Do you have the skills needed for a successful career in health care? One of the most important of these is communication. Good writing, speaking, and listening skills are essential. Your writing needs to be accurate and clear. Often workers need to record their experiences in short or long reports. Many employers complain that young people can text well, but they cannot write. Do you pay attention to grammar and mechanics? You also need to be able to speak clearly. How well can you explain a process to your peers? How well do others understand what you are trying to say? Equally important are your listening skills. You can learn so much from your patients by using active listening skills. It is important to ask questions to make sure you heard them correctly.

Different health care careers require different skills and abilities. You may have the right set of traits for one sector of the field but lack them for another. For example, you may have great people skills and a caring bedside manner. In this case, you might want to consider a career directly caring for patients. Some examples might be a nurse or a home health aide. On the other hand, you may be a whiz at technology and have the ability to follow detailed instructions. You might think about becoming an X-ray technician. If you are a good listener and problem solver, you might consider becoming a therapist or social worker. Looking at your strengths and weaknesses will help you figure out the right career for you.

How Can I Find the Right Role and Location for Me?

Taking the time to really explore the field of health care careers will pay off. It will help you find an occupation that fits your skills, abilities, and interests. A career that matches you well will provide a lifetime of rewards and job satisfaction. But how do you get there? There are many steps you can take and tools you can use to help you choose the right occupation.

A great place to start is at school. Your first stop might be your guidance counselor's office or your school's career center. There, you may be able to take an interest inventory. You will be asked questions about your interests, skills, and values. This inventory might suggest possible careers and educational and training options. It might even suggest occupations

Your school guidance counselor has many resources to help you choose a career, such as interest inventories, occupation and college search tools, and connections to job shadows and internships.

you had never thought about. Keeping an open mind may lead you to a perfect choice.

Your counselor or career technician may suggest that you try job shadowing. This is a chance to follow a health care professional or paraprofessional for a day and see the occupation up close. Interviewing various health care workers about their jobs can also give you insight into possible careers.

An internship is another way to look closely at a career. Interns get practical experience under the supervision of a qualified professional. An internship can last from a week to several semesters. Students gain valuable skills while learning what it's like to work in a specific career. Some internships even provide high school credit. For example, the John Muir Health System in northern California hires up to forty high school students each summer. These students get paid. They also get elective credit toward their diplomas. You might ask what internship programs your local hospitals offer.

There may be other opportunities to explore health care careers. For example, some colleges and universities hold special health care career fairs. Many colleges offer summer programs for high school students who are interested in health care careers. Your guidance counselor or career adviser can help you research your options.

What Else Should I Consider When Choosing a Career?

It is important to think about the amount of education or training you will need for your career choice. This will impact the pay you will receive and the lifestyle you can support. For example, becoming a home health aide may require just a few weeks of on-the-job training. These jobs are important, but workers usually don't make much more than minimum wage.

INTRODUCTORY HEALTH CARE CLASSES

You have signed up to take an Introduction to Health Care class. What can you expect? The class will include a history of health care. It will introduce the different career clusters, such as nursing, dental, and emergency medical careers, and the many jobs available within them. The class may include an introduction to anatomy and physiology, or the study of the systems of the body. Finally, it may teach some hands-on skills. You might learn to take someone's blood pressure. Or you might practice moving a patient from a stretcher to a bed. The instructor might show the class how to use a microscope. You might examine slides that have bacteria on them, for example.

In this class, you can discover what areas of the health care field you like. You may decide you prefer working with patients or that you enjoy lab work. Taking an introductory class can help you find a path to your future.

High school health care courses involve hands-on training, such as practicing taking a patient's blood pressure.

Students looking for more challenges—and income— should consider a career with greater training require- ments. With a strong start in high school and just a few months of training after graduation, students can work in many interesting health care careers. Some jobs include emergency medical technician (EMT) and phar- macy assistant.

Many students like school and look forward to two to four years of college. They might consider becom- ing a nurse or an imaging technologist. People in these positions are considered professionals. They typically make higher salaries than those without a college degree.

Many students say they would like to become a doctor, such as a surgeon or obstetrician. However, few students have the ability or money to spend eight to ten years in college and medical school. Only stu- dents with high scores on the medical school entrance exam, or MCAT, can find a spot in an American medical school. Colleges and medical schools also look at the rigor of the courses an applicant takes. If you want to consider a career as a medical doctor (MD), start by taking honors and Advanced Placement (AP) classes in high school.

How Can I Get a Good Foundation?

Regardless of what level of education you choose to pursue, you need to begin with a strong foundation.

Science, math, technology, and communication skills are the basis for any career in health care.

Good communication skills are essential. Take responsibility for weak reading and writing skills. Understand that these skills will determine whether you advance in your career or stay at a beginning level. Take advantage of every class that will improve these skills. Challenge yourself to read difficult materials. Read interesting stories about exciting breakthroughs in science and medicine. Put into practice all the steps in the writing process that your teachers having been teaching. In addition to your English classes, consider taking a speech class. Improving your speaking abilities will give you confidence in many situations.

Many students, even those who want to pursue a health care career, find science classes challenging. Biology, chemistry, and physics classes have difficult vocabulary and abstract concepts. There are several strategies you can use to do well in science. Science terms most often come from Latin and Greek. They share the same prefixes, suffixes, and root words. Making physical or digital flash cards can help you remember them. Pay attention to the visuals in your science books. Linking the diagrams and text in your mind can help you understand the concepts. The Internet also has many resources to help science students. You can find virtual dissections and interactive demonstrations. Entering a health care project in your school's science fair can make science fun. Finally, don't be afraid to ask your teachers for help. They often can explain difficult concepts in a way you can understand.

Science classes can be challenging, but learning to use high-tech tools such as microscopes can open up a whole new world.

Many students complain that they just don't get math. However, anyone can achieve in math classes with the right attitude and study skills. Becoming competent in math is like learning a language, playing an instrument, or becoming a top athlete. It requires constant practice. First, you need to do your homework every day. Each lesson is sequential, so a new concept builds on previous ones. It is important to do all the examples in the textbook. Your teacher can help you find your mistakes if you are careful to show all your work. Forming a math study group can be a big help, too. Your friends might have different approaches to problems that help you see them in a new way. Also check out Internet resources. You can replay tutorials on YouTube over and over again until you understand the process.

Having a good academic foundation in communication skills, math, and science will pay off in your future. A high grade point average will give you an edge in applying to career academies, magnet schools, and colleges. You will do better on placement tests such as the ACT, SAT, and Accuplacer. You can avoid taking remedial classes if you choose to go to college. And you will be prepared for the classes in your field of study.

Chapter Three

JUMPING INTO VO-TECH PROGRAMS IN HIGH SCHOOL

Are you ready to start working toward a career in health care now? Middle and high school students may be in luck. That career could start sooner than you think. There is a great need for health care workers. As a result, many cities are putting health care career programs in high schools. Some are called schools-within-a-school. Others are known as career academies. There are also magnet high schools that any student in the school district or region may attend.

The first place you should go to find out about programs and schools you may be interested in is your school's guidance office. Your counselor will be able to tell you what you might find in your area. Why should you consider a career academy or magnet school?

Students Do Better in High School

There are many reasons to think about attending one of these schools. One big reason is that students do better. According to an article in *USA Today*, students who focus on careers in specialized high schools such as career academies have better grades. They also have better test scores and graduation rates. They are

Middle school students learn about airborne diseases at a premedical career academy in Florida. Career academies and magnet schools can give students a head start on a rewarding career.

less likely to need remedial classes. The schools are effective because students apply the concepts they are learning using real-world cases.

These schools also weave health care lessons into all of their courses. Martha Lustik, staff member at the medical and allied health sciences magnet program at Washington High School in South Bend, Indiana, explains how: "We work hand in hand with their English and their biology and their Spanish. So when we're doing medical terminology in their courses in health science, they may be doing medical terminology in their Spanish. They all took medical Spanish because Spanish will give them a leg up in the medical community." This magnet program was featured in a story on WNDU in Indiana.

Students Get Experience in the Field

Students in career academies and magnet schools get field experience at health care sites. They can make lasting friendships with mentors in the area. Washington High School student Anthony Douglas shadowed a local obstetrician. "I've been able to assist in a pregnancy exam while I've been with him. Also, I've been in a couple of surgeries," Douglas told WNDU.

Fellow student Logan Francis had a similar experience. "Right now I am in an internship at Memorial Hospital. I am with a nurse in labor and delivery."

A magnet high school student takes a child's temperature in a pediatric ward. Students enrolled in health career programs get real-world experience with actual patients in local hospitals.

Another classmate, Emily Castro, wants a career doing medical research in a lab. She said, "They actually gave me an internship at Memorial Hospital for breast cancer research." Most high school health care programs have hospital partners for their students.

Students Earn College Credits

In many academies and magnet schools, students can earn college credits. This saves future tuition costs, which is helpful for students who plan on more education after high school. Often students take science and health care classes at local colleges. Some students graduate with as many as twenty-six college credits. Students also enter college with a clear idea of their major. "The opportunities we're presented, including mentorships, help make the decision of what to major in at college so much easier. It takes away a lot of the stress," Tina Chou, senior at the Academy of Allied Health and Science (AAHS) in Neptune, New Jersey, told the *Asbury Park Press*.

High School Graduates Can Get Jobs

In some programs, students can get credentials while still in high school. For example, students in the health technologies program at the Fairfield Career Center in Carroll, Ohio, graduate prepared for college. They are also ready for a good job. They complete a program that prepares them to become state-tested nursing assistants (STNA) and patient care assistants. Students that pass the tests can be hired at local hospitals.

Francisco Bravo Medical Magnet School in Los Angeles, California, has been identified by the U.S. Department of Education as a National Blue Ribbon School. It is located next to the Keck School of Medicine of the University of Southern California. The students are high achieving. Most of its graduates go on to college. They can help pay for college by working in their field. Qualified seniors can earn a CNA certificate and move right into a hospital job after graduation.

Academies, Schools-Within-a-School, and Magnet Schools: What's the Difference?

Health care academies and schools-within-a-school have become popular options in many school districts. Students may take core classes, such as English, social studies, and PE, with the rest of the high school students. Their electives are taken in the academy, which may be located on a different campus. Why would a student choose an academy or school-within-a-school instead of a magnet school?

An important reason for many students is that they can still participate in sports and extracurricular activities at their home high school. "You'll still be part of that school and join in those activities," said Kaitlyn Smathers of Fairfield Career Center, in a 2012 video

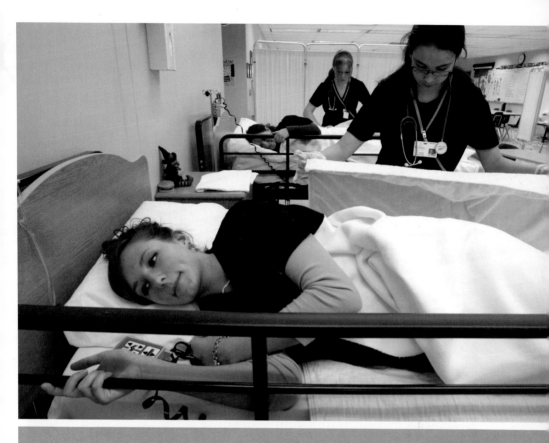

Students at a health career academy practice nursing skills, such as performing an occupied bed change, on each other.

promoting the school. She plays volleyball. Other Fairfield students participate in drama, debate, and clubs in their home high school.

Magnet high schools have one main focus, such as health care careers. They are usually open to anyone in the school district. They may be hard to get into. For example, in 2013, 1,600 students applied for 400

SKILLsUSA

If you enjoy competition, you might want to get involved with SkillsUSA. This club sponsors local, state, and national competitions in which students display their occupational skills. There are ninety-eight different skill areas. For example, in the first aid/CPR event, students are given an emergency scenario. They are graded on their ability to do procedures and take the best action. In the Health Knowledge Bowl, student teams compete to be the quickest to answer questions about the health care field.

In all events, winning students show leadership, teamwork, and a strong work ethic. "SkillsUSA has allowed me to be a better, more motivated person," said seventeen-year-old Ashley Dixon in an interview on the organization's Web site, SkillsUSA.org. "It's taught me the true values in life. Career-wise, it has trained me and given me all the qualities I need to get my job done right. I wouldn't change anything that I've learned for the world." Find out if your school participates in SkillsUSA.

ninth-grade spots at the Academy of Allied Health and Science in Monmouth County, New Jersey. Why choose a magnet high school? They often have more space devoted to the career. They may have labs and clinics. They may be located near a hospital. However, they may not have sports or clubs. There are also fewer opportunities to explore career areas outside of the health care focus.

There may not be enough spots in an academy or magnet school for all the students who want them. How can you improve your chances of getting into one? You will have to start planning as early as you can. You need to keep your grades high. You need to learn good study skills, including time management, note taking, and test taking. An interview may be required to get in. During the interview, you will need to impress the interviewer with your motivation. You will have to clearly state all the reasons the school is perfect for you. Students who are confident in their abilities will have an edge.

Taking Community College Classes

Another option for high school students is taking community college classes while still in high school. This may be a good choice for students in towns without academies or magnet schools in health care fields. Many high schools allow qualified students to take community college classes for dual credit. Students earn credit toward both their high school diploma and a community college degree or certificate. In some cases, students receive permission to spend half of the day off campus. During that time, they commute to their local college or a health care setting. In other cases, college classes are offered at the high school.

Students at the Academy of Arts, Careers, and Technology in Reno, Nevada, earn community college credits for some classes. These include EMT–First Responder and Medical Terminology.

In some places, high schools are located on college campuses. The high school students are mixed in with the college students. Thirty-five dual-credit Middle College High Schools (MCHS) operate in fourteen states. The goal is for high school students to earn a high school diploma. They also earn enough credits to equal one to two years of college.

Students who graduate from a Middle College High School may enter college with a year's worth of college credits already completed.

According to the Middle College National Consortium, in 2011, MCHS students earned an average of twenty-one college credits.

Most community colleges allow certain high school students to take classes. They can do this with or without dual credit. One key is scoring well on college placement exams. Many introductory health care classes have no prerequisites, so anyone can take them. However, other classes require high scores on reading and math entrance tests. Students can improve their chances of scoring well by studying ahead of time.

Making the Right Decision

If you live in a large city, you may have many educational options from which to choose in preparing for a health care career. Your school district may have both health academies and magnet schools. There may be a community college nearby with a strong allied health program. It may host a Middle College High School. Local hospitals might run their own entry-level training programs. With all of these opportunities, how does one choose?

If you want to participate in sports and extracurricular activities, then you'll probably want to attend an academy or a school-within-a-school. However, you might think that becoming completely immersed in career classes is more important. Then a magnet school or Middle College High School would be a better choice. These schools integrate career content throughout the whole program.

You might live in a school district without a health care career program or school. If so, you might consider a science, technology, engineering, and math (STEM) program or school. STEM programs provide a solid foundation in the science and math needed for a health care career. Health care professionals and paraprofessionals repeatedly stress the importance of this foundation for future success.

Finally, if there is no high school career program available, check with local hospitals and community colleges. There may be options for high school students before graduation. Volunteer opportunities, internships, or night classes may also give you the head start you need for your career in health care.

Chapter Four

LEARNING ON THE JOB WITH TRAINING AND CERTIFICATIONS

You have looked at the health care field and decided that a health care career would be a great fit. Maybe you have taken some health care classes in high school. You will soon be graduating. What else can you do to begin preparing for your future?

There are many options. Hospital apprenticeships are an important career entry path for many health care workers. Other workers, such as home health aides and medical assistants, may get on-the-job training through health care agencies or in physicians' offices. This training can lead to certifications. Physicians, dentists, podiatrists, and chiropractors in private practice may train high school graduates to become assistants or technicians. Many community colleges offer short-term programs in the allied health fields. Below you'll learn about careers that do not require a college degree.

Hospital-Based Apprenticeships

Many hospitals provide training for entry-level positions. These are typically support jobs on patient floors, in operating rooms, and in offices. Often the training combines classroom work with on-the-job learning. Sometimes students are placed in internships for more practice. For example, Partners Healthcare is a group of hospitals in the Northeast. It offers eight-week courses in many health care occupations. These include patient service coordinator, laboratory aide, and operating room assistant. The classes also teach students work and job-hunting skills.

A summer job in a hospital can be a great introduction to a health care career. Some hospitals provide summer jobs for teens. For example, Massachusetts General Hospital in Boston offers a summer youth jobs program. High school students work in units throughout area hospitals, such as in pharmacy, nursing, and research labs.

Kacthary Sanclemente was a medical assistant in the outpatient cancer center. In an interview on the hospital's Web site, MassGeneral.org, she gave advice to potential health care students. She said, "Be passionate about what you decide to do. It is not all about the money or what someone else sees you doing because it is something that potentially you will be doing for the rest of your life."

On-the-Job Training

If you have seen your doctor recently, you might have met his or her medical assistant (MA). This is the person who measured your height and weight and took your pulse and blood pressure. Maybe he or she asked some questions about your health. These medical assistants do important work for physicians. They are among many health care workers that are trained on the job in doctors' offices. MAs can work for optometrists, podiatrists, psychiatrists, and many other medical specialists.

What are some traits of successful medical assistants? First, they need good people skills. Patients may be anxious and in pain. MAs need to remain calm and patient. They must be able to learn to use clinical instruments such as a blood pressure cuff. They must be able to record patient information using a digital health record system. Successful MAs are very detail-oriented. They need to keep accurate records and be precise when recording patient data.

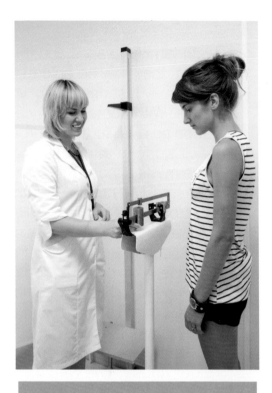

Medical assistants need excellent people skills, as well as the ability to take accurate measurements.

Another area in which employers often prefer training their own workers is home health care. The country's aging population has led to a boom in the need for home health care workers. Caring for elderly people in their homes has a lot of advantages. Seniors do better with familiar places and routines. In their home environment, they may be able to remain largely independent. They may just need help with meals, chores, and medications. With home health care, their health care dollars often go a lot further. Home health agencies can train their workers to do many tasks. For example, they can give medications. They can lift and move bedridden patients and help with bathing.

Home health aides (HHAs) also care for patients recovering from illness or surgery. They care for children and adults who need brief additional care. They also provide hospice care for patients who are terminally ill. "When I'm in home care, I'm a doctor, I'm a nurse, I'm a cook, I'm a dietician," home health aide Tracy Dudzinski told National Public Radio. "You name it, we do it."

One important role for HHAs is to watch out for elder abuse. The National Center on Elder Abuse says that one in ten senior citizens shows some signs of abuse. For example, they may be neglected. Their money may be vanishing. A key part of HHA education is learning how to spot and report abuse.

Becoming a home health aide offers many plusses for workers. The hours are flexible. Jobs are plentiful. Workers have the satisfaction of helping elderly or ill patients. However, there is a downside. Emptying bedpans and changing soiled sheets can be unpleasant. Confused patients or those in pain may not appreciate what the aide does. In addition it is one of the lowest-paying health care jobs. Unless they get more education, HHAs are likely to stay at the lowest rung on the career ladder.

Some communities offer programs for high school students and adults to learn high-demand jobs such as pharmacy technician.

Other workers who receive on-the-job training are pharmacy aides and lab assistants. Pharmacy aides train on the job to help the pharmacist. They may work the cash register, stock shelves, and answer phone calls. Completing insurance forms and entering patient data into the computer are other tasks. Lab assistants prepare blood and urine to be analyzed. They keep specimens organized.

CAREER LADDERS

High school is a great time to set career goals. Many health care workers start with an entry-level job. They only have a high school diploma. They then plan a step-by-step "ladder" to climb up to better-paying positions.

Here is an example. A high school graduate may study to become a CNA at a hospital or Red Cross office. He or she works at that job for a year or two, saving money. The person then takes classes at a community college to become a licensed practical nurse (LPN). Again, he or she works and saves money. The next step is finishing the classes to become an RN. The person keeps going to get a Bachelor of Science in Nursing (BSN) degree. Maybe he or she is still interested in more. The person goes back to school to become a nurse practitioner or physician's assistant. Or he or she decides to teach nursing classes. It may seem as if the sky is the limit. Before long, the individual is at the top of the profession.

It is hard to find the time and money to take classes. It is also hard to study for new certifications while working. Many health care employers want to help. They often give their workers time off for professional education. They may give tuition assistance or even provide tutors. This is a win-win for workers and employers. The workers get more skills and pay, while the hospitals get the trained staff they need.

Obtaining Certifications

Some employers are willing to train candidates for a position. Others may want workers to have certification. This proves to the employer that the candidate has completed a training program and passed a test from an accrediting agency.

There is sometimes more than one certifying agency in a field. This can become confusing. For example, there are four organizations in the United States that certify medical assistants. There are two that handle pharmacy techs. The Exam for the Certification of Pharmacy Technicians (ExCPT) and the Pharmacy Technician Certification Board Exam (PTCB) are given by different accrediting agencies. How do you know which certification to get? Once you begin taking courses, you will find out which exams most students take. Local employers will often prefer one.

Why is getting certification important? Your employer wants you to have certification for many reasons. Certification shows that an employee has the right skills to do the job. The employer knows that the job applicant has been well trained. Certification is also a plus for the employee. For example, a pharmacy technician will be given more responsibilities than a pharmacy aide. He or she will make more money, too.

It is important to seek certification from a trusted certifying agency. It is also important to take training classes from an accredited school or program. Accreditation shows that an institution has met certain standards for its program. Finding out if a particular school or training program is accredited can be challenging.

PREPARING FOR TESTS

Students in the health care field often complain about the amount of studying they have to do. There are quizzes and tests, midterms and finals. Then there are the certifying exams, which can be hours long. In some cases they are offered only once or twice a year. They can cost a lot of money.

What can you do to do well on tests? In an interview on the Web site ExploreHealthCareers.org, nursing student Cam Hawkins explained his strategy: "I knew it was going to be rigorous. But I did not expect so much reading. I am a very slow reader. So I really have to plan ahead to get everything studied."

Here are some other strategies. First, don't cram. It is stressful, and it is not effective. You might remember some facts for the test, but you will forget them soon afterward. A better idea is to prepare for a test far in advance. Put definitions on flash

Making flash cards and reviewing over a long period of time will help you recall information when you need it.

cards. Carry them around and review them often. Create possible short-answer and essay questions. Write simple outlines of the answers. Reviewing material over a long period of time puts the information into long-term memory.

Do not stay up the night before the test trying to memorize information. This doesn't work. Your brain uses sleep to organize information. With proper sleep, you will be alert during your test. You will be able to confidently choose the best answer for each question.

One program in an institute may be accredited but another may not. For example, a school may be known for its accredited business program. Then it may add a dental assisting or massage therapy program. These may not be accredited. One place to look is the school's Web site. There you will have to look very carefully to find information about accreditation.

Be careful about enrolling in online schools or programs. An online class cannot take the place of clinical practice. Certificates in most fields require a certain amount of supervised time spent with patients. An accredited school will require a student to spend a lot of time in a clinic or hospital setting. There might be a few exceptions, such as programs for medical coding and billing.

One trusted training organization is the American Red Cross. You might already have taken some classes through this organization, such as first aid,

CPR, lifeguard training, or babysitter's training. In some communities, the Red Cross also offers first responder and emergency medical response courses. These prepare students to take the National Registry Exam for emergency medical responders (EMRs). Its nurse assistant training classes prepare students for the CNA exam.

Short-Term Training Programs

There are a variety of other certifications for which one can train in the health care field. Students can take short courses that enable them to earn certification but do not lead to a college degree. These can be found in vocational schools, career colleges, and community colleges. For example, the Maricopa Skill Center in Phoenix, Arizona, is housed at Gateway Community College. It offers a two-week assisted living caregiver program and a four-week EKG technician certification program. It also offers a twenty-five-week ophthalmic assistant program, among others. To qualify for these programs, students need to have a high school diploma or GED.

Another short course is for emergency medical technicians (EMTs). Candidates need to be at least eighteen years old. They need to complete a course of 110 hours and then pass an exam. Their job is often exciting. They drive or ride along in an ambulance and respond to emergency

Community colleges, hospitals, and fire departments offer emergency medical technician (EMT) courses for students who want an exciting, fast-paced career.

calls. They stabilize patients. Then they transport them to hospitals. Individuals can receive training from hospitals, fire departments, or community colleges. Another place to get EMT training is the Job Corps program. This is a free, federally funded program for low-income students. Participants need to be at least sixteen years old. Job Corps has 125 locations nationwide.

Phlebotomists draw blood from patients for testing. The in-class requirement typically is forty hours of instruction. Students then complete forty hours of supervised clinical practice. Once the training is finished, students need to pass a national exam. They can then find jobs in hospitals, labs, and blood banks.

There are many ways to get health care certifications, from going through hospital training to taking courses at Red Cross centers and community colleges. Candidates can also train on the job. Then they can take a qualifying exam. All of these are great ways to move up in the health care world.

Chapter Five

THINKING ABOUT COLLEGE? YOU CAN DO IT!

As you can see, a rewarding health care career can be possible for you. You do not necessarily need a college degree. Career education in high school, on-the-job-training, short courses, and certifications can get you a good job. You can work in hospitals, care facilities, labs, and offices.

However, you may find that you want more pay and a higher-level job. Then you will need to think about earning a college degree. An associate of science in nursing (ASN) degree can be earned at a community college, junior college, or vocational school, often in two or three years. Some students might want to go further in the profession. They can study for a bachelor of science in nursing (BSN) degree at a university.

There are many factors to consider when looking at a college degree. What kind of student are you? What are your long-term goals? How much money do you have for school? Where will you go for more education? How do you decide which type of college will be the best for you? Here are some things you might want to think about.

Community Colleges Offer Value in Higher Education

There are probably many colleges in your area. These might be public colleges, which include junior colleges, community colleges, and state colleges and universities. Tuition tends to be less at public schools than at private or for-profit colleges. In general, junior and community colleges have half the tuition cost of four-year colleges and universities. Graduates of community colleges will find that their degrees and credits are accepted at universities in their state. They provide good value for a student's tuition dollars. However, there are often too few spots in popular programs for all the students who want them.

What kind of health care programs can you find at a community college? One of the biggest community colleges in the United States is Miami Dade College in Florida. It gives degrees and certificates in twenty health care areas, from nursing to dispensing optician. Even very small community colleges have health care programs. For example, Otero Junior College in Colorado offers degrees and certificates for nurses, nursing assistants, and massage therapists. Students can usually complete a certificate program in one year. An associate's degree usually takes two years or more.

Nursing Programs

The most popular program at most community colleges is nursing. The shortest nursing program is the

A nursing student listens to the breathing of an automated dummy at West Virginia State Community and Technical College. Nursing programs are among the most popular offerings at community colleges.

one to become a licensed practical nurse (LPN), sometimes called a licensed vocational nurse (LVN). Students can complete the LPN program in a year. These nurses work under the direction of RNs. LPNs who want to get licensed take the National Council Licensure Examination for Practical Nurses (NCLEX-PN).

Students who want to become RNs apply for a two-to-three year nursing program. Like the LPN programs, the RN program combines classroom study with clinical practice. Students earn the associate degree in nursing (ADN). Before they can work, nurses must pass the National Council Licensure Examination for Registered Nurses (NCLEX-RN).

Nursing schools can be hard to get into. Many community colleges have two to three times more students applying than the number for which they have room. Only the top students get in. Students need high grades on prerequisite courses in math, science, and general education. Sometimes scores on the ACT or SAT are considered. It also helps to have volunteer experience.

How can students improve their chances of getting into nursing school? High school students can look for summer programs between high school graduation and college. These are often called bridge programs, pipelines, or career pathways. These programs focus on improving students' basic skills in reading, writing, and math. There is usually a study skills component to help students improve their time-management, goal-setting, note-taking, and test-taking skills. Once in college, students need to work hard on the prerequisites. They can form study groups and take advantage of college tutoring programs to help them succeed. Even getting a B instead of an A can hurt one's chances of getting into the nursing program.

Nursing school applicants should pay attention to detail when filling out their applications. Many applications are rejected because they are incomplete or contain errors. An important part of many applications is the personal statement. This is like a short essay. Here students can explain why they want to be a nurse. Colleges use this statement to gauge motivation. It also acts as a writing test. This is the time to show strong writing skills. A complete, accurate, well-written application also shows an ability to follow directions. It can improve a student's chances for acceptance into the program.

Many hospitals prefer that their nurses have a BSN in addition to an RN. This degree includes more training in communication, critical thinking, and leadership. Student nurses spend time in a wide variety of settings outside of hospitals. Colleges often have special programs for those with ASNs to complete their BSNs.

Considering For-Profit Schools

An Internet search of colleges offering health care programs in your area may turn up a long list. You may even see ads for for-profit schools. These are businesses whose goal is to make money for their investors. For-profit schools can be a good choice for some students. Their programs are more intense and go faster. They may be easier to get into. However, they cost more. According to a 2012 U.S. Senate report, associate degree and certificate programs at for-profit colleges cost about four times as much as those at community colleges and public universities. Some of the schools have very low graduation rates and high dropout rates. Some schools' credits are not accepted at public colleges if students want to transfer to get their BSN. You may be considering a for-profit school. Make sure you do a lot of research to find out if the school has any of these problems.

Whatever schools you are considering, there are some important questions to ask. You can research the information or ask school representatives. By looking at the answers, you can compare the

Attending a college fair is a great way to find a school that will meet your needs.

schools. Putting the answers into a chart can be helpful. Key questions include the following:

- What is the total cost of the program?
- What is the graduation rate?
- What percent of graduates get jobs in their field?
- What is the cost of transportation to get to the college?
- What are the admission requirements?
- How hard is it to get accepted into the program I want?

Here are some additional questions to ask yourself:

- Are my skills strong enough to be successful at this college?
- Can I pay for the program, or will I have to take out loans?

Answering these questions honestly will help you avoid failure and years of debt and will allow you to choose the best school to achieve your goals.

Financial Aid Can Provide Money for College

Many high school students would be surprised at how many college students get financial help in paying for college. According to a report from the National Center for Education Statistics, 85 percent of first-time college

WORKING AS A PHYSICAL THERAPY ASSISTANT

Would you ever think of spending time in a swimming pool as part of your job? You might if you are a physical therapy assistant (PTA). A pool is just one of the places a PTA can help a patient heal. PTAs do a wide variety of tasks. Their days are never the same. They work in hospitals with heart or cancer patients. They help the patients learn to use their muscles the way they did before surgery. They help patients in wheelchairs learn to be independent. PTAs also work with children in schools. They often turn the tasks into games to make them fun. Playing catch is a great way to improve a child's hand-eye coordination, for example. Many community colleges and vocational schools have PTA programs. Most PTAs have an associate's degree.

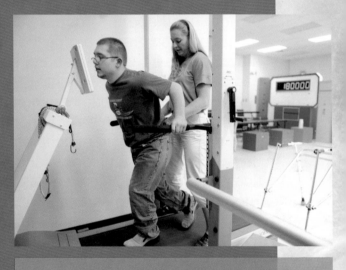

Physical therapy assistants help patients with conditions such as cerebral palsy improve their muscle function so that they can walk independently.

students receive some sort of financial aid. This percentage is even higher at for-profit colleges. Some of this money is in grants, which do not need to be paid back. Most financial aid is in the form of loans. Students need to start paying back loans when they are finished attending the college. Let's look at the different kinds of financial aid.

Grants and Scholarships

Grants are often called "free" money. The U.S. Department of Education offers a variety of grants. These are based on financial need. The amount you get depends on your need and the cost of attending the school. The most common grants are called Pell Grants. Colleges may also have their own sources of grant money they can give to qualified students.

Scholarships are another source of financial aid that does not have to be repaid. Schools offer scholarships. They can also come from nonprofits, religious institutions, companies, employers, and professional organizations. Most scholarships are based on merit or ability. They are awarded to students with high grades and test scores. They are also given for athletic achievement, musical talent, and contributions to the community. Students should never pay a service to find scholarships. There are many free sources of scholarship information.

Loans and Work-Study Programs

A loan is borrowed money that needs to be paid back, with interest. There are many places from which students can get loans. The biggest lender is the U.S. government. It offers many types of education loans, depending on a student's need. Some are low-interest loans, subsidized by the government. This means that the government offers a lower interest rate than a bank. Students usually need to start paying back loans six months after they graduate or stop going to school. Loans need to be paid back even if the student doesn't graduate or complete the program.

Another option students have in paying for college is the work-study program. Colleges help students find part-time jobs on campus. Sometimes local nonprofit and public agencies offer jobs as well. The federal government pays part of the students' wages. The work-study program is for students who demonstrate financial need.

Applying for Financial Aid

The first place you should go if you want information on financial aid is the school's financial aid office. All students applying for financial aid need to fill out the Free Application for Federal Student Aid (FAFSA) form. This application can be completed online. You and your parents should complete the form together. The amount of aid you receive depends mostly on your parents' income. They will need their Social Security numbers and federal tax returns.

If you or your parents have never filled out the FAFSA before, it can be confusing. However, that is not a reason to avoid the form. There is plenty of help available. You can do a live chat with online support staff. The

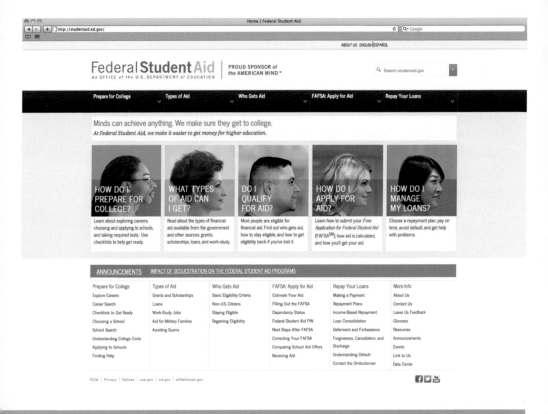

The Federal Student Aid Web site (http://studentaid.ed.gov), sponsored by the U.S. Department of Education, offers easy-to-understand information about applying for financial aid for college.

financial aid officers at the college you want to attend can also help.

After you have applied to a college, the school will let you know, based on the FAFSA form, how much financial aid you can get. Usually students get a combination of grant and loan money, and possibly work-study.

Some students refuse to think about taking out loans for college. They do not want to get into debt. They may worry about their ability to pay the loans back. It is true that student loan debt in the United States is very high. However, in many cases, taking out a loan can be a good choice. Moving from a CNA to an LPN or RN will significantly increase your pay. So will moving from an aide with on-the-job training to an assistant or technician with an associate's degree. You will need to do your research. You need to find an affordable school with a good job placement rate. Then you can be confident you will be able to pay back your loans.

There are many career paths in health care. All of them can provide rewarding jobs. To choose wisely, you need to know yourself. You need to find the right occupation for your personality and abilities. You need to explore all your training and education options. You need to put energy into making sound plans. With these steps, you can achieve your goals. You can have a great career in health care.

Glossary

accredited Officially recognized as meeting the essential academic requirements.

acute Extremely great or serious; critical; severe.

apprenticeship A program in which an inexperienced person works for a skilled worker to learn a trade.

arthritis A disease that causes the joints to become inflamed and painful.

blood pressure The pressure of blood against the inner walls of blood vessels.

chronic Continuing for a long time or recurring frequently.

credential A document that shows that a person is qualified to do a particular job.

diagnostics The science and practice of identifying a disease or condition.

dialysis A process in which uric acid and urea are removed from a patient's blood, which is then returned to the patient's body.

dietician A person who is an expert in nutrition.

dual credit Relating to a course or program whose credits apply to both a high school diploma and a college degree.

hospice A program of care and support for the terminally ill.

imaging The use of instruments to obtain pictures of the inside of the body.

internship A formal program to provide practical experience to beginners in an occupation.

mentor A person who teaches or gives advice and support to a less experienced person.

obstetrician A doctor who specializes in delivering babies and caring for women before and after they give birth.

ophthalmic Pertaining to the eye.

optometrist A medical professional that diagnoses disorders and diseases of the visual system, prescribes corrective lenses, and treats eye diseases or refers them for treatment.

outpatient A patient who receives treatment in a hospital but does not stay the night.

paraprofessional A trained aide who assists a professional such as a doctor.

podiatrist A medical professional that diagnoses and treats disorders and diseases of the foot.

post-traumatic stress disorder (PTSD) A psychological condition that can affect a person who has experienced a highly stressing event, such as wartime combat or a natural disaster. It is usually characterized by depression, anxiety, flashbacks, nightmares, etc.

prerequisite Something required beforehand, such as a course that is required before taking an advanced course.

recession A period of decline in the economy when business activity, employment, and earnings fall below normal levels.

residential care Long-term care given to patients who live in a facility, rather than at home.

sequential The following of one thing after another in a regular order.

ultrasound The application of high-frequency sound waves to create an image of the inside of the body.

For More Information

The College Board
45 Columbus Avenue
New York, NY 10023-6992
(212) 713-8000
Web site: http://www.collegeboard.org
The College Board is a not-for-profit organization
that helps students plan for, research, apply to,
and pay for college. It also helps students prepare for college entrance and placement exams.

HOSA—Future Health Professionals
548 Silicon Drive, Suite 101
Southlake, TX 76092
(800) 321-HOSA (4672)
Web site: http://www.hosa.org
This organization encourages leadership and
health care career skills by sponsoring programs,
competitions, and local and national conven-
tions. There are HOSA chapters in high schools,
technical schools, community colleges, and
universities.

Institute for Broadening Participation (IBP)
P.O. Box 607
Damariscotta, ME 04543
(866) 593-9103
Web site: http://www.ibparticipation.org
This organization aims to increase diversity in the
science, technology, engineering, and mathemat-
ics (STEM) workforce. It designs and implements
strategies to increase access to STEM education,

funding, and careers, with special emphasis on diverse, underrepresented groups.

Job Corps
U.S. Department of Labor
200 Constitution Avenue NW, Suite N4463
Washington, DC 20210
(202) 693-3000
Web site: http://www.jobcorps.gov
Job Corps provides housing, training, and education for eligible young adults. There are 125 locations where students can choose from 100 careers. Students also receive help with independent living skills and employability skills.

Service Canada
Youth Employment Strategy
Canada Enquiry Centre
Ottawa, ON K1P 0J9
Canada
(800) 935-5555
Web site: http://www.servicecanada.gc.ca
The Youth Employment Strategy is the government of Canada's commitment to help young people get the information and gain the skills, work experience, and abilities they need to make a successful transition into the labor market.

Skills Canada
294 Albert Street, Suite 201
Ottawa, ON K1P 6E6

Canada
(877) 754-5226
Web site: http://www.skillscanada.com
Skills Canada promotes careers in skilled trades and technologies by supporting regional and national events and competitions. Students also learn about and practice employment skills.

SkillsUSA
14001 SkillsUSA Way
Leesburg, VA 20176
(703) 777-8810
Web site: http://www.skillsusa.org
SkillsUSA is a partnership of students, teachers, and industry working together to ensure America has a skilled workforce. This organization sponsors competitions in which students demonstrate occupational and leadership skills. It promotes teamwork, self-confidence, and character development. Students join SkillsUSA at their schools.

Web Sites

Due to the changing nature of Internet links, Rosen Publishing has developed an online list of Web sites related to the subject of this book. This site is updated regularly. Please use this link to access the list:

http://www.rosenlinks.com/TRADE/Health

For Further Reading

Adney, Isa. *Community College Success: How to Finish with Friends, Scholarships, Internships, and the Career of Your Dreams.* Bedford, IN: NorLights-Press, 2012.

Barker, Geoff. *Health and Social Care Careers.* Mankato, MN: Amicus, 2011.

Boles, Blake. *Better Than College.* Loon Lake, CA: Tells Peak Press, 2012.

Chandler, Genevieve E. *The Ultimate Guide to Getting into Nursing School.* New York, NY: McGraw-Hill, 2008.

DeLaet, Roxann. *Introduction to Health Care & Careers.* Baltimore, MD: Lippincott, Williams & Wilkins, 2012.

Getting Financial Aid 2014. New York, NY: The College Board, 2014.

Gray, Kenneth. *Getting Real: Helping Teens Find Their Future.* Thousand Oaks, CA: Corwin Press, 2009.

Makely, Sherry, Shirley Badasch, and Doreen Chesebro. *Becoming a Health Care Professional.* Upper Saddle River, NJ: Prentice Hall, 2013.

McCormick, Lisa. *Financial Aid Smarts: Getting Money for School* (Get Smart with Your Money). New York, NY: Rosen Publishing, 2012.

Morkes, Andrew. *Hot Health Care Careers: More Than 25 Cutting-Edge Occupations with the Fastest Growth and Most New Positions.* Chicago, IL: College & Career Press, 2011.

Naik, Anita. *Beat Stress! The Exam Handbook* (Really Useful Handbooks). New York, NY: Crabtree Publishing, 2009.

Porterfield, Jason. *Frequently Asked Questions About College and Career Training* (FAQ: Teen Life). New York, NY: Rosen Publishing, 2009.

Rowh, Mark C. *Community College Companion: Everything You Wanted to Know About Succeeding in a Two-Year School.* Indianapolis, IN: JIST Publishing, 2011.

Sommer, Carl. *Teen Success in Career and Life Skills.* Houston, TX: Advance Publishing, 2009.

Snyder, Thomas. *The Community College Career Track: How to Achieve the American Dream Without a Mountain of Debt.* Hoboken, NJ: John Wiley & Sons, 2012.

Strange, Cordelia. *Medical Technicians: Health-Care Support for the 21st Century.* Broomall, PA: Mason Crest Publishers, 2010.

Stratford, S. J. *Field Guides to Finding a New Career: Health Care.* New York, NY: Infobase Learning, 2009.

U.S. Department of Labor. *Young Person's Occupational Outlook Handbook.* 7th Ed. Indianapolis, IN: JIST Publishing, 2010.

Vinik, Debra, and Joshua Halberstam. *The Community College Guide.* Dallas, TX: BenBella Books, 2009.

Wilson, Patrick, and Scott McEvoy. *Health IT JumpStart: Best First Step Toward an IT Career in Health Information Technology.* Hoboken, NJ: John Wiley & Sons, 2012.

Wischnitzer, Saul, and Edith Wischnitzer. *Top 100 Health-Care Careers.* Indianapolis, IN: JIST Publishing, 2011.

Bibliography

Anderson, Chris. "U.S. Will Need 5.6 Million More Health-care Workers by 2020." *Healthcare Finance News*, June 27, 2012. Retrieved June 26, 2013 (http://www.healthcarefinancenews.com/news/us-will-need-56-million-more-healthcare-workers-2020).

Bilmes, Linda. "Soldiers Returning from Iraq and Afghanistan: The Long-Term Costs of Providing Veterans Medical Care and Disability Benefits." Kennedy School of Government, Harvard University, 2007. Retrieved June 27, 2013 (http://www.hks.harvard.edu/fs/lbilmes/paper/Bilmes_vacostwar_010707.pdf).

Boyd, Alesha Williams, and Michelle Gladden. "More Students Turn to Career Academies." *USA Today*, May 27, 2013. Retrieved June 30, 2013 (http://www.usatoday.com/story/money/business/2013/05/27/career-academies-find-seat-in-schools/2364421).

Cherry, Donald, Christine Lucas, and Sandra L. Decker. "Population Aging and the Use of Office-Based Physician Services." National Center for Health Statistics, Centers for Disease Control and Prevention, August 2010. Retrieved June 27, 2013 (http://www.cdc.gov/nchs/data/databriefs/db41.PDF).

Eastland-Fairfield Career & Technical Schools. "High School – Programs – Health Technologies." 2012. Retrieved July 15, 2013 (http://www.eastland-fairfield.com/HighSchool/programs/healthTechnologies.aspx).

ExploreHealthCareers.org. "Q&A with Nursing Student Cam Hawkins." May 6, 2008. Retrieved July 30, 2013 (http://explorehealthcareers.org/en/

profiles/student/Article/175/QA_with_nursing_
student_Cam_Hawkins).

Federal Interagency Forum on Aging-Related Statistics. "Older Americans 2012: Key Indicators of
Well-Being." 2012. Retrieved June 27, 2013 (http://
www.agingstats.gov/agingstatsdotnet/Main_Site/
Data/2012_Documents/Docs/EntireChartbook.pdf).

Georgetown University Center on Education and the
Workforce. "With or Without Obamacare, the United
States Will Need 5.6 Million More Healthcare Work-
ers by 2020, Georgetown University Study Says."
June 21, 2012. Retrieved June 27, 2013 (http://
www9.georgetown.edu/grad/gppi/hpi/cew/pdfs/
Healthcare.PressRelease.pdf).

Goldstein, Dana. "The Future of Vocational Education." *The Nation*, April 19, 2012. Retrieved December 16, 2013 (http://www.thenation.com/
blog/167476/future-vocational-education#).

John Muir Health. "Exploring a Career in Health
Care." 2013. Retrieved July 30, 2013 (http://
www.johnmuirhealth.com/get-involved/careers/
exploring-a-career-in-health-care.html).

Ludden, Jennifer. "Home Health Aides: In Demand,
Yet Paid Little." National Public Radio, October 16,
2012. Retrieved July 14, 2013 (http://www.npr
.org/2012/10/16/162808677/home-health-aides
-in-demand-yet-paid-little).

Martin, Patti. "A Day in the Life of Academy of Allied Health and Science." *Asbury Park Press*,
December 19, 2008. Retrieved July 14, 2013
(http://www.app.com/article/20081219/

LIFE/81217038/A-day-life-Academy-Allied-Health
-Science?nclick_check=1).

Massachusetts General Hospital. "MGH Summer Alumni Program Q&A." November 7, 2011. Retrieved July 8, 2013 (http://www.massgeneral.org/about/newsarticle.aspx?id=3114).

McFadden, Maureen. "Washington High School's Medical Magnet Program Healing the Future." WNDU.com, September 28, 2012. Retrieved July 15, 2013 (http://www.wndu.com/news/specialreports/headlines/Washington-High-Schools-Medical-Magnet-program-healing-the-future-171816121.html).

Middle College National Consortium. "College Readiness." 2013. Retrieved July 14, 2013 (http://www.mcnc.us/our-data/college-readiness).

Monmouth County Vocational School District. "Welcome to Allied Health and Science." June 27, 2013. Retrieved July 14, 2013 (http://www.aahs.mcvsd.org/index2.html)

myFootpath.com. "Certified Nursing Assistant Career Interview." 2011. Retrieved July 31, 2013 (http://myfootpath.com/career-advice-and-answers/career-interviews/certified-nursing-assistant-career-interview).

National Center for Education Statistics, U.S. Department of Education. "Financing Postsecondary Education in the United States." May 2013. Retrieved July 19, 2013 (http://nces.ed.gov/programs/coe/indicator_tua.asp).

National Center on Elder Abuse. "Red Flags of Elder Abuse." 2013. Retrieved July 16, 2013 (http://

www.centeronelderabuse.org/Red%20Flags%20
of%20Elder%20Abuse.asp).

Partners Healthcare. "Partners in Career and Workforce Development." 2013. Retrieved July 8, 2013
(http://www.partners.org/For-Employees/PCWD/
Exploration/Health-Care-Training-And-Employment/
Default.aspx).

Quinton, Sophie. "This Isn't Your Dad's Vocational
School." NationalJournal.com, December 7, 2013.
Retrieved December 16, 2013 (http://www
.nationaljournal.com/next-america/education/this
-isn-t-your-dad-s-vocational-school-20131216).

Simon, Stephanie. "Obama Calls for Focus on Vocational Training." Reuters, February 13, 2012. Retrieved December 17, 2013 (http://www.reuters
.com/article/2012/02/13/us-usa-budget
-education-idUSTRE81C1Z620120213).

SkillsUSA. "SkillsUSA Champions – Summer 07."
2007. Retrieved July 19, 2013 (http://www
.skillsusa.org/champions/2007_Summer/
feature1_ashley.html).

U.S. Bureau of Labor Statistics. "Health Care – BLS
Spotlight on Statistics." November 2009. Retrieved
June 27, 2013 (http://www.bls.gov/spotlight/
2009/health_care/home.htm).

U.S. Bureau of Labor Statistics. "Veterinary Technologists and Technicians." *Occupational Outlook Handbook, 2012–13 Edition*, March 29, 2012. Retrieved
September 1, 2013 (http://www.bls.gov/ooh/
Healthcare/Veterinary-technologists-and-technicians
.htm#tab-4).

U.S. Department of Education. "Federal Student Aid."
2013. Retrieved July 18, 2013 (http://studentaid
.ed.gov).

U.S. Department of Education. "Innovations in Education: Successful Magnet High Schools." September
2008. Retrieved July 15, 2013 (http://www2
.ed.gov/admins/comm/choice/magnet-hs/report
_pg17.html).

U.S. Senate Committee on Health, Education, Labor,
and Pensions. "For-Profit Higher Education: The Failure to Safeguard the Federal Investment and Ensure
Student Success." July 30, 2012. Retrieved July 8,
2013 (http://www.help.senate.gov/imo/media/for
_profit_report/PartI-PartIII-SelectedAppendixes.pdf).

U.S. Department of Veterans Affairs. "Health Care."
2013. Retrieved June 27, 2013 (http://www.va.gov).

Workforce3 One. "Allied Health Occupations for
Young Adults Podcast Series: Certified Nursing
Assistant/Certified Home Health Aide (Tran-
script)." September 19, 2011. Retrieved July
18, 2013 (https://www.workforce3one.org/
view/2001126251236611895/info).

Index

About the Author

As a high school and community college instructor, Susan Henneberg has over thirty years' experience assisting teens and young adults in beginning successful careers in a wide variety of occupations. She has trained hundreds of educators in methods to encourage the critical thinking, motivation, and self-discipline students need to achieve their dreams. She teaches and writes in Reno, Nevada.

Photo Credits

Cover (figure) Bevan Goldswain/Shutterstock.com; cover (background), pp. 1, 3 EPSTOCK/Shutterstock.com; p. 5 John Moore/Getty Images; p. 8 Jackson Hole News & Guide/Price Chambers/AP Images; p. 10 Jupiterimages/Polka Dot/Thinkstock; p. 13 Sun Sentinel/McClatchy-Tribune/Getty Images; pp. 14–15 John Slater/Stone/Getty Images; pp. 18–19 Kathryn Scott Osler/The Denver Post/Getty Images; p. 22 The Washington Post/Getty Images; pp. 24, 48, 50–51, 55, 61 © AP Images; p. 27 Jupiterimages/Stockbyte/Thinkstock; pp. 30–31 © The Palm BeachPost/ZUMA Press; p. 32 © Augusta Chronicle/ZUMA Press; p. 35 © Brendan Fitterer/Tampa Bay Times/ZUMA Press; p. 38 © U-T San Diego/Zuma Press; p. 43 Iakov Filimonov/iStock/Thinkstock; p. 45 Benjamin Lowy/Getty Images; pp. 58–59 Michael S. Gordon/The Republican/Landov; cover and interior elements PinkBlue/Shutterstock.com (x-ray), Jirsak/Shutterstock.com (tablet frame), schab/Shutterstock.com (text highlighting), nikifiva/Shutterstock.com (stripe textures), Zfoto/Shutterstock.com (abstract curves); back cover graphics ramcreations/Shutterstock.com; Palsur/Shutterstock.com (caduceus icon).

Designer: Michael Moy; Editor: Andrea Sclarow Paskoff; Photo Researcher: Amy Feinberg